THE PERFECT STORM

A Memoir

By:

MARKIANA CORNIST

i

DEDICATION

***

To God, who carried me through every storm I thought would break me.
To my daughter, my reason, my strength, and one of God's greatest gifts in my life.

To my mother, whose love, prayers, and support never failed me. And to every woman walking through her own storm right now *trust Him. He is not finished with you yet.*

"Trust in the Lord with all thine heart; and lean not unto thine own understanding.
In all thy ways acknowledge him, and he shall direct thy paths."
Proverbs 3:5–6

ACKNOWLEDGEMENTS

***

First and foremost, I give all glory and honor to God. None of this would exist without Him. Thank you, Lord, for carrying me through every storm, for strengthening me when I was weak, for correcting me when I needed direction, and for loving me even when I did not fully understand your plans. This story is living proof that you never leave us, even in our darkest moments.

To my daughter, thank you for being my reason to keep going when life felt heavy. Your love, your presence, and simply being your mother have been among God's greatest blessings in my life. You gave me purpose in seasons when I felt lost, and I thank God for you every single day.

To my mom, thank you for your prayers, your support, and your unwavering love. You stood beside me in moments when I felt as though I could not stand on my own. Your strength and support has carried me more times than I can count, and I will forever be grateful.

To my pastor, thank you for your guidance, your prayers, and for being obedient to God's voice. Your leadership, wisdom, and encouragement strengthened my faith and pushed me to keep going even when things felt impossible. I am deeply grateful for the covering, truth, and spiritual direction you provided during one of the most pivotal seasons of my life.

To my family, friends, and all those who encouraged me, prayed for me, and spoke life into me during difficult seasons, thank you. Your words, your presence, and your support mattered more than you may ever know.

And finally, to every woman who has ever felt broken, overlooked, ashamed, or uncertain about her future, this book is for you. May my story remind you that storms do not come to destroy you. Sometimes, they come to reveal who you truly are.

TABLE OF CONTENTS

Dedication III

Acknowledgements IV

Introduction VIII

Growing Up 1

Becoming A Mother 7

Student Nurse 13

Fulfilling My Purpose 17

Still… Wanting More 22

The Calm Before The Storm 27

The Storm Begins… 33

Uncertainty 38

The Day Everything Changed 45

Brace Yourself 52

My New Reality 60

Trying Again 67

The Storm Continues 75

The Breakup 83

Reality Set In 90

Pain, Purpose, Strength 97

Commit Thy Way 107

What The Storm Revealed 113

INTRODUCTION

***

There are storms in life that arrive without warning.

They don't ask permission. They don't wait until you're ready. They come suddenly, shifting everything you thought was stable, unraveling plans you carefully built, and forcing you into places you never imagined you would have to stand.

This book is not just a story about hardship.

It is a story about transformation.

It is about what happens when life no longer looks the way you planned, when control slips through your hands, and when God begins to rebuild you in ways you didn't ask for but desperately needed.

Every chapter you are about to read is real. Every emotion, every decision, every loss, every moment of growth happened in real time, often without understanding why.

But what I learned is this:

Storms are not always sent to destroy you.

Sometimes, they are sent to reveal you.

To expose what was never solid.

To strip away what cannot go with you.

To strengthen the parts of you that comfort never could.

If you have ever felt broken, confused, disappointed, or unsure of what God is doing in your life, this book is for you.

My prayer is that as you read, you don't just see my story, you see yourself. And more importantly, you see God.

Because even in the middle of the storm, He is still present. Still working. Still faithful.

And He is not finished with you yet.

1

GROWING UP

***

I had a good childhood.

That is where my story begins, and that is what makes everything that followed harder to explain.

My mother raised three children. Two she gave birth to, and one she inherited through loss. When my grandmother passed away, my uncle Jeff was only nine months old. My mother stepped in and raised him as her own. To the outside world, he was my uncle. Inside our home, he was my brother. He called my mother *"Mom,"* and I never knew him any other way.

For the first five years of my life, I was an only child. When Jeff came to live with us, our family expanded not through chaos, but through responsibility and love. My mother carried that responsibility with quiet strength, even when it weighed on her. Years later, when I was thirteen, she had my younger brother, Keith. That made me the only girl, tucked between two boys, protected and seen.

I grew up feeling secure. Loved. Covered. There was structure in our home. There were expectations. There was discipline. I did not feel neglected or overlooked. My childhood was not perfect, but it was steady. And for a long time, I believed steady meant safe.

High school became one of the happiest seasons of my life. I was involved, social, and confident in who I was becoming. I danced on the dance team, modeled in school fashion shows, and became known as the genuinely nice girl who could dress. In my senior year, I was voted *Best Dressed* and named *Homecoming Queen*.

I had identity. I had affirmation. I had direction.

When it came time to choose a college, I decided to attend one about forty minutes from home. It felt like the perfect distance, far enough to taste independence, close enough to retreat if I needed to. I moved onto campus full of anticipation, ready to step into adulthood.

College was exciting, but underneath the excitement was caution. I watched the sororities and fraternities stroll. I attended campus events. I went to a few parties, but I never fully relaxed there. I studied people. I observed how alcohol transformed them, how loud they became, how different they acted once their inhibitions dissolved. It unsettled me.

I did not drink then. I did not want to lose control of myself. I did not want to wake up and not recognize who I had been the night before. Discipline had always protected me. I believed if I stayed disciplined, I would stay safe.

During my first Christmas break home from college, I spent one day with my ex-boyfriend. We were no longer together. It wasn't planned. It wasn't dramatic. It was just one day that felt familiar, comfortable, unfinished.

I returned to campus in January shortly after my nineteenth birthday. Classes resumed. Life resumed.

But something felt different.

When my cycle did not come, I tried to ignore the quiet fear rising inside me. I told myself it was stress. Adjustment. Anything but what my mind kept whispering. Days passed. The whisper grew louder.

Eventually, I bought a pregnancy test.

I remember standing in the small dorm bathroom, staring at the white stick in my trembling hand. The room felt too quiet. Too still. I told myself not to overreact. I told myself I would handle whatever came.

When the lines appeared, I felt the world shift.

The first emotion was not fear. It was not shame. It was disappointment.

Deep disappointment in myself.

I had been careful. I had been disciplined. I had built my identity on self-control and good decisions. And now, one choice had altered everything. We were not even in a relationship anymore. There was no plan. No conversation about a future. Just a moment that could not be undone.

I sat there longer than I needed to, staring at the test, feeling the weight of consequence settle over me. I whispered a quiet prayer I did not even fully know how to form. *God, what have I done?*

Telling my mother was one of the hardest conversations of my life. Her disappointment cut deeper than any fear I had felt alone in that bathroom. I understood her reaction. That almost made it worse. I had always wanted to make her proud. Her approval mattered to me. And now, I felt as though I had cracked something fragile between us.

Still, she showed up.

For a while, I remained on campus. I attended classes. I moved through hallways as if nothing had changed.

But everything had changed. I was carrying something I had not planned, something that required maturity I did not feel ready for.

Then one day, everything stopped.

I was lying in my dorm bed when a sharp pain tore through my body. It was sudden and consuming. I tried to sit up, but I couldn't. My limbs felt heavy. My thoughts blurred. Fear rose fast and violently.

I called my mom, crying, telling her something was wrong. I could barely form the words. She told me to get to my car and meet her at my doctor's office back home.

I do not remember the full drive. I remember gripping the steering wheel. I remember praying under my breath. *Please, God. Please.*

When I arrived at the doctor's office, the pain had not subsided. It pulsed through me in waves. After examining me, the doctor said I needed to go to the hospital immediately.

On the way there, I vomited.

And then, almost instantly, the pain eased.

My body felt different. Lighter. Calmer.

I did not yet understand what had happened, but I understood that something inside me had shifted.

In that moment, lying between fear and relief, I realized something deeper than the physical pain.

I was not as independent as I believed. I was not as in control as I imagined. Discipline alone could not shield me from consequence or uncertainty.

Before anyone suggested it, before conversations about school resumed, I knew I did not want to return to that university.

I wanted to go home.

I wanted my mother.

I wanted to cover.

For the first time, I understood that safety was not a location. It was a surrender.

And I was about to learn what surrender would truly require.

2

BECOMING A MOTHER

***

My pregnancy was spent surrounded by my mom, friends, and family. Even though my life had changed quickly, I wasn't alone. They made sure I felt loved, welcomed, and seen. In a season that could have felt isolating, their presence steadied me. I learned that love can hold you upright when everything else feels uncertain.

I was small-framed, so watching my belly grow felt almost miraculous. Each week, my body stretched in ways I had never imagined. I documented every stage. I took pictures. I stood in front of the mirror and studied the quiet transformation. I still dressed up. I still showed up as myself. I refused to let shame shrink me. Even though I was walking this road alone, I allowed myself to enjoy being pregnant.

Before I even knew the gender, I kept saying I was having a girl. It wasn't something I analyzed. It was something I felt. Every time I said it, someone would laugh and tell me, *"You're going to have a boy because you keep saying girl."* But deep down, I knew.

At twenty weeks, I went to the appointment alone.

The room was dim, quiet except for the soft hum of the ultrasound machine. I lay there watching the screen, searching for outlines I barely understood. When the technician smiled and confirmed it, I felt it before she said it.

It's a girl.

I was right.

Tears filled my eyes, not from surprise but from certainty. I whispered her name in my heart before I ever said it aloud. In that moment, even without anyone sitting beside me, I didn't feel abandoned. I felt chosen. I felt entrusted.

Her father had entered another relationship at the beginning of my pregnancy, so he wasn't around. That truth hurt more than I allowed myself to admit at the time. I drove myself to appointments. I sat in waiting rooms alone. I celebrated milestones quietly. He didn't attend the baby shower. Each absence was a small confirmation that I would have to be stronger than I had planned to be.

There were nights I cried. Not loudly. Not dramatically. Just quiet tears that fell while I lay in bed thinking about how different I had imagined this would be. But every morning, I woke up and kept going. I didn't have the luxury of falling apart. I had a daughter to prepare for.

When I went into labor, he was there. He drove me to the hospital and stood in the room when she arrived three and a half weeks early, weighing six pounds and eight ounces. When they placed her in my arms, everything else faded.

I named her Mariah.

That day did not just change my life. It redefined it.

I was nineteen years old and officially a mother. I didn't know how to be one. There was no blueprint. No instruction manual. No certainty that I would get it right. But when I looked at her, something settled inside me. Fear did not disappear, but it no longer led. Responsibility did.

While I was pregnant, I worked at a daycare center, and I stayed there until Mariah turned one. Being around children every day felt like preparation. I was learning patience, structure, and attentiveness. I didn't realize it then, but God was training me in the ordinary.

When Mariah was two, I was hired at a hospital as a patient transporter. Around the same time, I enrolled in community college. I knew I wanted to finish school. I just didn't know who I was becoming yet.

At first, I chose sonography. It looked interesting, and at that stage of my life, interesting felt like enough.

Working at the hospital felt natural. I transported patients to rooms, testing areas, and discharge. But more than that, I talked to them. I listened. They told me their fears, their frustrations, their hopes. I found myself lingering when I could, offering small reassurances I wasn't technically required to give. My coworkers were kind, and for the first time in a while, I felt stable.

But stability stirred something deeper.

I wanted to do more than move patients from place to place. I wanted to care for them.

One day, a nurse stopped me and said, *"You should become a Patient Care Assistant. You have the presence for it. The heart for it."*

Her words stayed with me.

When I learned the hospital would pay for the classes, I felt something shift. Opportunity rarely knocked twice in my life. I wasn't going to ignore it.

So I signed up.

The classes ran Monday through Friday from 8:00 a.m. to 4:30 p.m. for two weeks straight. To make it work, I temporarily switched to night shifts, working from 6:30 p.m. to 3:30 a.m. It was the only option.

Logistically, it was complicated. Emotionally, it was harder.

I had to arrange for someone to take Mariah to and from daycare and keep her during the week. For two weeks, I would only see her on the weekends.

The first night I dropped her off, I held her longer than usual. She didn't understand why I was leaving. She just waved and smiled. I got in the car and cried before I even pulled away.

Those two weeks were some of the most exhausting of my life. I functioned on minimal sleep. I studied during breaks. I worked through the night. I missed my daughter constantly. The house felt too quiet without her small footsteps. I questioned myself more than once.

But every time doubt crept in, I reminded myself why I started. This was not about convenience. It was about building something stronger than my circumstances.

Growth does not always announce itself loudly. Sometimes it looks like a sacrifice that no one sees.

When I completed the program and became a Patient Care Assistant, something inside me became clear. This was more than a job. It was alignment. I felt useful in a way that felt purposeful, not accidental.

That was when I knew nursing was not just an option. It was a calling.

I changed my major from sonography to nursing.

Looking back now, I realize that decision was the first time I stopped reacting to life and started responding with intention. It was the first time I stepped into purpose instead of simply surviving.

And I did it not because everything around me was stable, but because I decided to become stable within it.

3

STUDENT NURSE

***

While I was working as a Patient Care Assistant, I was also attending school, completing my nursing prerequisite classes. On the days I didn't have class, I worked. On the days I didn't work, I studied. And every single day, regardless of the schedule, I was a mother.

My life revolved around balance. Responsibility. Provision. Progress.

In the mornings, I moved with purpose. Packing lunches. Dropping my daughter off at daycare and reviewing notes in the quiet spaces between responsibilities. At night, after dinner was cooked and homework was done, I studied until my eyes grew heavy. Some nights I fell asleep over my books. Other nights, I whispered prayers before turning another page.

Once I completed all of my prerequisite courses, I applied to the nursing program. The waiting period felt longer than it probably was. I tried not to dwell on it, but I knew what that acceptance would mean. It wasn't just school. It was access to a different future.

A few weeks later, I opened the letter.

I stood in the kitchen, my daughter nearby, her small voice filling the room. My hands trembled slightly as I unfolded the paper. When I saw the word *"Congratulations,"* I paused. Not because I didn't understand it. But because I did.

I had worked for that moment and prayed for it. Sacrificed for it.

I was genuinely happy, but beneath that happiness was something else—a quiet awareness. Nursing school would change my life, but only temporarily. I understood that the season ahead would be demanding, intense, and all-consuming. There would be no room for distraction.

The nurses I worked with had already warned me.

"You have to eat, sleep, and breathe nursing," they said.

I believed them.

I knew my social life would disappear. I knew there would be invitations I couldn't accept and moments I would miss. And yet, I felt no resentment. I wasn't chasing comfort. I was chasing stability. I was building something that would outlast the season of sacrifice.

The same month nursing school began; I received a letter approving me for housing assistance.

When I read it, I didn't call it luck. I didn't call it a coincidence.

That was God.

The timing was too precise. I already knew I would have to reduce my work hours to survive academically. I knew I could not do both at full capacity. That support arrived exactly when I needed it. It wasn't excessive. It wasn't an abundance. It was enough.

Enough to breathe.

Enough to focus.

Enough to keep going.

Once school started, my world narrowed, but not in a way that felt restrictive. It felt purposeful.

My focus was on two things: my daughter and my education.

While friends traveled and posted pictures of celebrations and vacations, my days followed a steady rhythm. Daycare drop-off. Class. Pick-up. Dinner. Bath time. Study. Repeat.

There wasn't extra money for anything beyond what was necessary. If there was spending to be done, it was for my daughter. I paid my bills. I kept food in the refrigerator. I showed up to class prepared. That was the standard.

There were nights when exhaustion settled into my bones. Nights when I questioned whether I was stretching myself too thin. Nights when I sat quietly after my daughter fell asleep and asked God for strength, not for the future, but just for the next day.

Discipline didn't announce itself as strength at the time. It felt like survival. It felt like doing what had to be done without applause, without recognition, without ease.

But looking back, I see it differently.

That season was forming something in me that textbooks could not teach. It was teaching me endurance, focus, and faith without spectacle.

I didn't realize it then, but nursing school wasn't just preparing me for a career.

It was preparing me for life.

4

FULFILLING MY PURPOSE

***

The day I finished my last exam in nursing school; I sat in my car for a long time before turning the key in the ignition.

My hands were still shaking from the test. My mind replayed questions I wasn't sure about. But beneath the nerves, there was something else rising slowly in my chest.

It was over.

I did it.

The tears came quietly at first, then all at once. Not dramatic. Not loud. Just steady. Every late night of studying after my daughter went to sleep. Every sacrifice. Every moment, I wanted to give up, but I didn't. Every time I questioned whether I could really make it through.

Some endings don't feel like endings. They feel like proof that you didn't quit.

Graduation carried a joy I had earned. When I walked across that stage, I felt the weight of everything it took to get there.

I wasn't just receiving a degree. I was holding evidence of discipline, obedience, and endurance.

My parents were proud. My family celebrated. My friends showed up. My daughter looked at me with a smile that felt bigger than the room. That smile meant more than any applause.

For the first time in a long time, I allowed myself to sit in that feeling without rushing past it. I let myself feel proud. I let myself breathe.

But there was still one more hurdle ahead.

The nursing boards exam became my final test of perseverance.

I took it the first time and walked out unsure. When the results came back, and I saw that I had failed, I stared at the screen longer than I needed to. My heart sank, not because I believed I wasn't capable, but because I wanted it so badly. I had already imagined the relief of being done.

I told myself it was okay. I would try again.

The second time felt heavier. I studied harder. Prayed longer. Walked in determined. When I failed again, the tears were different. They weren't just disappointed. They carried embarrassment. Fatigue. A whisper that asked, *"What if this isn't for you?"*

I didn't want to admit that thought, even to myself.

I remember sitting alone and asking God why the door hadn't opened yet. I had done the work. I had stayed disciplined. I had obeyed when it was hard. Why was this part so difficult?

Looking back now, I understand that delay does not mean denial. But in the moment, delay feels personal.

The third time, I approached it differently. I made flashcards and carried them everywhere. I practiced questions until I could see patterns. I studied with intention instead of anxiety. And I prayed, not just for a passing score, but for peace.

I reached a point where I told God, *"I have done what I can. The rest is in Your hands."* That surrender did not come easily. It came after frustration. After tears. After wrestling.

When I found out I passed, I fell to my knees on the floor of my room. Not gracefully. Not ceremoniously. Just overwhelmed.

"Thank you," was all I could say.

The room felt quiet and sacred. I wasn't just relieved. I felt seen. The journey had stretched me, disciplined me, and humbled me. And now it had produced fruit.

I was officially a nurse.

And that was when things began to change.

A few days later, I received a job offer. When I saw the salary, I stared at the number for a moment, almost afraid to believe it. It wasn't just income. It was stability.

For the first time, I could save without fear. I could provide without calculating every dollar twice. I remember standing in the grocery store one evening, placing items in my cart without anxiety, tightening my chest. I bought something extra for my daughter just because I wanted to. That small moment felt like freedom.

Financial stability wasn't about money alone. It was about peace.

Most importantly, I was doing work that mattered. I cared for patients during some of their most vulnerable moments. I listened. I comforted. I advocated. Caring for people was not just my profession. It felt like a purpose.

There was fulfillment in showing up for others. In being present. In knowing that my obedience had led me here.

I had worked hard. I had endured a delay. I had trusted when I didn't understand.

And now I was standing in the life I had prayed for.

What I did not yet realize was that success does not exempt you from storms.

Sometimes, it prepares you for them.

5

STILL... WANTING MORE

***

While working as a nurse, I served in many different settings. Eventually, I found myself in home care, providing one-on-one support inside a client's home. The client's mother was kind and welcoming. The stepfather was not. Some days, the tension in that house was thick, but I stayed. I stayed because I needed the stability. I stayed because the pay was good. And over time, I stayed because endurance had become second nature to me.

That job gave me something I had never truly experienced before: flexibility. It also gave me financial breathing room. For the first time in my adult life, I was not surviving. I was building.

With a predictable schedule and steady income, my world began to expand. I traveled. I saved money. I bought cars. I checked off quiet dreams I had carried for years. On the outside, my life looked full. In many ways, it was.

By the time I turned thirty-one, I felt ready to buy my first home.

The house was beautiful. Four bedrooms. A finished basement. Two living rooms.

A two-car garage. An above-ground pool that shimmered in the summer sun. During the pandemic, when the world felt uncertain, I added a jacuzzi to the deck. It felt like control. Like security. Like a reward.

Little by little, I updated the bathrooms, replaced the carpet, and installed new flooring. Each change made it feel more personal. More rooted. More ours.

That house became a gathering place. I hosted family and friends often. My mom began hosting gatherings there, too. Her friends started calling it the *"vacation house"* because of the pool and the jacuzzi. Laughter filled the rooms. Music echoed down the hallway. The scent of food drifted from the kitchen into every corner.

I did not just buy a house. I created space. I created joy.

And yet, somewhere beneath the gratitude, something else quietly grew.

Contentment and craving can live in the same heart.

I had everything I once prayed for, but I started imagining more. More space. More grandeur.

A larger closet. An upstairs balcony overlooking the living room. Higher ceilings. A layout that felt elevated.

I told myself it was growth.

I did not ask myself whether it was restlessness.

In my second year living there, I contacted my realtor and said I was ready for something bigger. I had accumulated more clothes over the years, but if I am honest, it was not just about closet space. It was about expansion. About reaching the next level. About proving, perhaps even to myself, that I could.

I secured my preapproval from the bank and began scrolling through listings with anticipation. But it was a seller's market. Homes disappeared before I could even schedule a showing. Offers soared far above the asking price.

Instead of seeing that as a pause, I saw it as opposition.

So, I pivoted to new construction.

A new build meant no bidding wars. No competition. Just patience and paperwork.

When my realtor and I visited the subdivision, I found it almost immediately. High ceilings.

A massive closet. An upstairs overlooking the living room. It looked like the vision I had been carrying in my head.

I felt certain.

I placed my current home on the market and received multiple offers. I chose a family that felt right. After closing, I used the equity as a down payment for the new build.

While construction began, my daughter and I moved in with my mom. The building process became sacred in a way I had not anticipated. We visited the site often, watching wooden beams rise from foundation to frame.

Before the drywall went up, we wrote Bible verses on the exposed wood of our rooms. The scent of fresh lumber surrounded us as we pressed ink into raw beams. We prayed over empty spaces. We asked God to dwell there. To protect it. To bless it.

In that moment, it felt holy.

There were obstacles during the process. Delays. Paperwork complications. Minor financial hiccups. Each one required effort to resolve. Instead of asking whether the resistance meant to slow down, I interpreted it as something trying to block my blessing.

I pushed harder.

I prayed, but my prayers sounded more like negotiations than surrender.

After four months of construction, we closed in the fifth month, on December 6, 2022.

I remember walking through the finished home. The smell of new paint. The echo of our footsteps on untouched floors. The way my voice carried differently in the high ceilings.

I moved my clothes into the large closet I had imagined for months. I stood there for a moment longer than necessary, running my hand across empty shelves that would soon be full.

Mariah was excited. We welcomed the new year inside the walls we had watched rise from nothing. It felt aligned. Timed. Orchestrated.

I told myself this was a favor.

And maybe it was.

But peace built on circumstances can shift just as quickly as circumstances do.

At the time, I believed I was stepping into expansion.

I did not yet realize I was stepping into a storm I could not see.

6

THE CALM BEFORE THE STORM

***

The year 2023 began beautifully.

I traveled to Mexico, settled into our new home, and allowed myself to finally exhale. For the first time in a long time, life felt light. Stable. I wasn't bracing for impact. I wasn't scanning the horizon for the next wave. I was simply living, enjoying the fruit of the hard seasons I had already survived.

I thought the storm was behind me.

In April, a man named Chris commented on one of my Facebook stories. I had posted a workout video, and he said I had motivated him to go work out. I responded politely but briefly. I wasn't interested in entertaining anyone. I had learned the cost of misplaced trust.

A couple of weeks later, he commented again, this time asking how long I had been a nurse. It was a simple question, but something about the consistency made me pause. I clicked on his profile and actually looked.

He was handsome, yes. Muscular. Tattoos lining his arms. But what caught my attention wasn't just his appearance. It was the photos of him with his child. The way he spoke about God—the steadiness in his presence.

That mattered to me.

This time, I responded differently.

Our conversations grew. Messages turned into phone calls. Phone calls turned into plans. And before I realized it, we were meeting in person.

We met for the first time on *Cinco de Mayo,* May 5. He arrived straight from work, still in his uniform, carrying a plant and knockout roses. It was such a small gesture, yet it disarmed me. He wasn't flashy. He was intentional.

Conversation flowed easily. We laughed. There was no performance. No pressure. Just ease.

After that first date, everything accelerated. We saw each other nearly every day. He brought roses often, never making a show of it—just quiet consistency. I wasn't used to that kind of gentleness.

If I'm honest, I wasn't ready for a relationship. Not emotionally. Not spiritually. I was still healing from my past.

There were moments I felt guarded, even sharp in my responses. At times, I was unintentionally unkind. I didn't know how to receive steady love without questioning it. I didn't know how to relax into something that didn't feel chaotic.

Sometimes we walk into the very thing we once prayed for, only to realize we have to grow into it.

Still, it unfolded.

On June 4, 2023, I visited his church for the first time. The atmosphere felt different from what I was used to. It was intimate. Unified. There was a closeness among the people that I couldn't ignore. It was Apostolic, something unfamiliar to me, but I kept returning.

Later that month, we traveled to Las Vegas and stayed at the *Wynn*. It felt surreal. He met my family, who lived there, and they loved him immediately. Watching him blend into my world so naturally felt comforting. Effortless.

Life felt aligned.

On July 30, during a service I had attended several times before, something shifted.

I received the Holy Ghost.

I didn't fully understand what was happening in the moment. I only knew that I felt overcome in a way that wasn't emotional hype or pressure. It was deeply personal, as if something within me had awakened. As if God had stepped closer than I ever allowed Him before.

I left that service feeling marked. Changed in a way I couldn't yet articulate.

By August, I began waiting for my cycle, but it never came. Instead, there was only light spotting. I tried to ignore it at first. I didn't want to assume anything. I had been told years earlier that my body wasn't capable of carrying another child.

In 2020, after my fibroid surgery, my doctor flushed my tubes during the procedure and found them blocked. At my follow-up appointment, he told me gently but clearly that another pregnancy was unlikely.

I grieved that quietly back then.

So, on August 6, 2023, when I took a pregnancy test and saw *pregnant* appear across the screen, my body went still.

I stared at it longer than necessary, as if blinking might erase it.

Then I broke down.

Not just tears. Deep, shaking sobs.

Shock. Gratitude. Fear. Hope. All of it collided at once. It felt like God had rewritten a sentence I thought had already been finalized, like he had crossed out the word *impossible* and written *miracle* over it.

I called Mariah downstairs and showed her the test. She cried immediately. She had been asking for a sibling since she was four years old. Now she was fourteen, standing in front of me with tears streaming down her face, thanking God.

When Chris came over, I told him the news. He hugged me tightly, steady as always. After a moment, he said, *"We have to get married."*

It didn't feel forced. It felt like alignment.

I was happy. I was excited. I found myself watching my stomach in the mirror, already imagining life forming inside me. I allowed myself to dream.

But something felt unsettled.

The spotting didn't stop. And there was a persistent pain in my lower left side. Not sharp enough to panic, but present enough to whisper.

I tried to silence it. I wanted joy to be louder than concern.

Still, unease crept in.

So, I called my doctor and scheduled an appointment.

That was when everything began.

7

THE STORM BEGINS...

****

I had already scheduled an appointment with an OB-GYN, but I couldn't wait for it. I was still spotting, and the dull ache in my lower left side had not eased. It wasn't sharp, but it was persistent, like a quiet warning I couldn't ignore. Something didn't feel right. So I went to the emergency room.

The waiting room felt colder than usual. I remember sitting there, holding my purse in my lap, trying to steady my breathing. I kept telling myself it could be normal. Women bleed in early pregnancy sometimes. I repeated that to myself like a prayer.

They examined me and confirmed that I was bleeding. They ran a pregnancy test. When it came back positive, I felt a flicker of relief. At least I wasn't imagining it. At least it was real.

Because of the bleeding, they performed an ultrasound.

When the doctor returned, his expression was careful. He told me they didn't see a sac. He said it was likely I would miscarry.

The word *miscarry* echoed louder than anything else he said. I felt my chest tighten. Tears came before I could stop them. I wasn't ready to lose something I had only just begun to believe in. I had already started imagining another car seat, another set of tiny clothes folded into drawers, another heartbeat in our home.

Not long after, Chris arrived. I could see the concern in his eyes before he even spoke. Then another doctor came in, an OB-GYN. Her tone was calmer, steadier. She explained that it might simply be too early to see anything on the ultrasound. She said they would monitor my HCG levels and referred me to an OB-GYN office for follow-up care.

Her words gave me something to hold onto.

That day, they sent me home.

I left the hospital with confusion, but also with hope. Hope can feel louder than fear when you want something badly enough. I clung to the possibility that this was just timing, just uncertainty, just a test of patience.

The next day, I went to my OB-GYN appointment. I was still bleeding. They performed an internal ultrasound in the office. The room was dim, and the only light came from the screen. The technician pointed to it.

"There," she said softly.

I saw it, the sac.

Relief rushed through me so quickly that it almost made me dizzy.

But then she grew quiet.

She explained that the sac was irregular in shape, and that irregular sacs often ended in miscarriage. Her voice was gentle, but the words still felt heavy. They told me they would continue monitoring my HCG levels.

Every two days, my levels doubled, just like a normal pregnancy.

I held onto that. I watched the numbers like they were promises. I prayed constantly. Not elaborate prayers, just simple ones: *"God, please. Please let this work."* I believed He could turn it around. I believed He had the final say.

I watched my belly slowly begin to round. I took pictures every day, documenting what I hoped would become proof of a miracle. For the first time in years, it felt possible that I could give my daughter the sibling she had asked for over the past ten years. I let myself imagine her excitement. I let myself imagine the announcement.

On August 13, 2023, I returned to the hospital because the pain had worsened. It was sharper now, more concentrated on my left side. I could no longer convince myself it was nothing.

This time, when they performed the ultrasound, they wouldn't let me see the screen.

I noticed it immediately.

The technician adjusted the monitor away from me. The room felt quieter than before. I asked if I could look. She told me it was their policy.

It hadn't been their policy before.

A weight settled in my stomach. Something in the atmosphere had shifted, even before anyone said a word.

After the ultrasound, the doctor came in. His tone was serious but measured. He explained that the pregnancy appeared to be implanted in the wrong place. He used the term *ectopic pregnancy.*

I didn't fully understand what that meant at first. I had walked into the hospital, preparing myself for a possible miscarriage. I didn't realize I was stepping into something more dangerous, something that could threaten my own life.

They explained I would need to be admitted for further care.

By then, my mom and Chris had arrived. I could see fear in their faces, though they tried to hide it. I was admitted directly from the emergency room and taken upstairs.

As I lay in the hospital bed, the fluorescent lights humming above me, everything felt suspended. Nervous. Sad. Deeply confused. I had prayed. I had believed. I had watched the numbers double. I had allowed myself to hope.

Now I didn't know what was going to happen next.

I only knew that everything I had been building my faith around suddenly felt fragile.

8

UNCERTAINTY

***

When I arrived at the unit, the nurse told me I couldn't eat. They didn't yet know what the doctors were going to do, and it was already late. Chris stayed the night with me, and my mom went home. I barely slept.

Hospitals have a way of stretching time. The lights never fully dim, the sounds never fully stop. I lay there listening to machines hum and footsteps echo down the hallway, wondering how something that had started with such quiet hope could now feel so uncertain.

The next morning, Chris left for work, and the doctors came in.

They told me my pregnancy was an extremely rare type of ectopic pregnancy called a *cervical ectopic pregnancy.* It was life-threatening and accounted for less than one percent of ectopic pregnancies. The doctor explained that they didn't have hands-on experience treating it. They had read about it in school, but they were still determining the best course of action.

In that moment, I realized I was entering unknown territory, not just for me, but for them.

There is a particular kind of fear that comes when even the experts do not speak with certainty. My hands felt cold as they explained the risks. I nodded as if I understood everything, but inside I was spiraling. I wanted someone to say, *"We know exactly what to do."* Instead, I heard words like consult, research, and discuss.

They told me they were meeting as a team, reviewing options, weighing outcomes. I was admitted for three days. During the first two, they came into my room with different plans, different possibilities. One of those possibilities was a hysterectomy.

That word did not leave me.

Hysterectomy.

It echoed in my mind long after they left the room. I thought about what it meant. The finality of it. The closing of a door I had not even fully stepped through. I thought about future birthdays, future pregnancies, possibilities I had not yet named. I felt something inside me tighten, not just fear of surgery, but fear of loss beyond this loss.

Throughout those days, family and friends came to visit. They sat beside my bed. They held my hand. They prayed. Their presence meant more than they knew.

I was surrounded, yet I felt incredibly alone inside my own body. My body had become the battleground, and I did not recognize it.

One day, an African American caseworker came to check on me. She sat down gently, asked how I was really doing, and offered resources. Her tone was not rushed. It was not clinical. It was human.

The following day, she returned with a small plant and a card. She told me she was sorry I was going through this and shared that her sister had experienced something similar. She said she would pray for me.

That broke me.

I had been trying to stay composed, answering doctors' questions, nodding at treatment plans, trying to be strong. But her kindness slipped past my defenses. I cried in front of her, quiet, steady tears that I had been holding back. In the middle of so much uncertainty, her compassion felt like a lifeline from God Himself.

On the second day, the doctors came to a decision. They would treat the pregnancy with *methotrexate*, two injections, one in each hip.

Methotrexate is a low-dose chemotherapy medication. It stops the pregnancy from continuing to grow and allows the body to absorb the tissue.

I listened carefully as they explained the process. I signed forms. I tried to detach from the reality of what was happening.

They told me I would need to return in two days for bloodwork to check whether my HCG levels had decreased.

After the injections, I was discharged.

I left the hospital feeling sad. Confused. Hollow.

I kept asking God why. Not angrily. Just quietly. Why this? Why now?

Two days later, on a Thursday, I returned to the hospital to have my blood levels checked. I went to the triage unit, where pregnant women were arriving to give birth. I sat there quietly, hands folded in my lap, watching life move forward around me.

Women walked in holding their bellies. Families carried balloons. Nurses moved with purpose.

I felt invisible.

When the woman at the front desk checked me in, she asked for my name and date of birth. Then she asked for my due date.

I told her I did not know.

She looked at the screen and said I was due on *April 11, 2024.*

April 11, 2024.

Hearing it spoken aloud made it real in a way it had not been before. A day that would now come and go like any other. I broke down crying.

She immediately apologized and explained that it was part of the check-in process. I told her I understood. I did. But knowing the date, knowing what would never be hit me harder than I expected.

When I was taken back to the room, the doctor entered with my lab results. My HCG levels were still rising, doubling like a normal pregnancy.

They told me they would administer two more methotrexate injections and check my levels again in two days. If they did not decrease significantly, a hysterectomy would be necessary.

I said no.

The word came out before I fully processed it.

I was not ready to accept that outcome attached to my body. Not yet. I did not know whether that response was faith or fear. I only knew I was not prepared to surrender that part of myself without exhausting every other option.

The doctor explained gently but firmly that it would be life-saving. If the pregnancy continued, I could hemorrhage. I could die.

Death. Loss. Surgery. Finality.

I left the hospital that day crying, hurt, overwhelmed, and terrified.

The following morning, I received a phone call from Dr. O. He told me he usually did not call patients directly; residents typically handled follow-ups, but he wanted to check on me personally.

His voice was steady.

He said he did not want to scare me, but if I experienced any bleeding after the injections, I needed to come to the hospital immediately.

"This is life-threatening," he said.

I told him I understood. I told him I had not seen any bleeding, just a small piece of tissue. He told me to save his number.

I did.

And then I went about my day, carrying grief I did not yet know how to name. Somewhere beneath the fear, beneath the questions, beneath the word hysterectomy echoing in my mind, I whispered a prayer I could barely form.

God, keep me.

That was all I had.

9

THE DAY EVERYTHING CHANGED

***

Saturday came, August 19, 2023, and I felt normal.

There was nothing in the air that warned me. No heaviness. No intuition. Just an ordinary morning.

I sat at the dining room table eating breakfast, talking on the phone with Chris while he worked overtime. We talked about small things. When we hung up, I called my mom. She was at the mall, checking out at a store, and said she would call me right back.

I finished eating, rinsed my plate, and walked to the refrigerator for something to drink. Then I went to the bathroom.

That was when everything changed.

I looked down and felt my chest drop. My pad was full of blood.

For a second, my brain refused to process it. I just stared. Then the fear came in fast and sharp.

Not again.

Please, God, not again.

My hands started shaking as I reached for my phone. I called my mom.

She answered and said, *"Markiana, I'm checking out, I'll call you right back."*

"Mom," I said, my voice already breaking, *"I am bleeding."*

There was a pause. I could hear it in her silence before she spoke again. Her tone shifted immediately.

"Leave now. Meet me at the hospital."

I tried to stand.

Blood poured out of me onto the toilet, onto the floor. It was more than spotting. More than heavy bleeding. It was uncontrolled. I couldn't even get dressed. Every time I moved, more came.

I felt panic rise in my throat. I knew what this could mean.

My mom called back and realized I was still home. She began yelling that I needed to leave, but I physically couldn't. There was too much blood.

She called Chris. They called an ambulance.

I stood there waiting, holding onto the counter, trying to breathe through the fear. I kept whispering, *"God, please. Please. Please."*

When the ambulance arrived, the EMTs came inside and checked my vitals. They asked if I could walk out to the stretcher.

"I can walk," I said.

Even as I said it, I felt weak.

I walked outside and sat down on the stretcher. The drive to the hospital felt strangely calm. The EMT kept checking my vitals and making conversation, almost casually. I answered her questions, but inside, my thoughts were racing.

Is this it?

Am I losing my baby right now?

I was wearing black pants with white drawstrings. By the time we arrived at the hospital, the white strings were soaked red.

They rushed me through the emergency entrance and into a room.

My mom was already there. My dad came. My aunt. Chris. They all waited outside. I could see the fear in their faces before the door closed.

The doctor ran in. She said they had expected me to be unconscious from the amount of blood I had lost, but I wasn't. I was fully aware. Fully present.

They removed my sweatpants. When they saw the extent of the bleeding, the room shifted into urgency.

"If we can't stop this," the doctor said, *"we will have to take you back immediately for an emergency hysterectomy."*

The word *hysterectomy* echoed in my mind.

My mom dropped her head and began crying.

I felt like the air had been pulled out of the room.

No more children.

No more chances.

And I had just finally become pregnant again.

After everything. After the waiting. After the prayers. After daring to hope.

I didn't cry at first. I went still. Completely still. My body felt like it didn't belong to me anymore. Like I was watching it happen from above.

Doctors gathered, including Dr. O, moving quickly to create a plan to stop the bleeding without removing my uterus. They administered medication typically used for severe hemorrhaging.

Time stretched. Minutes felt like hours.

At some point, I stopped asking God to fix it.

Instead, I prayed differently.

"Lord, whatever happens, I trust You. Even if I don't understand it. Even if it breaks me."

That prayer didn't come easily. It felt like surrendering something I desperately wanted to hold onto. But I knew obedience meant trusting Him even here.

After hours, the bleeding finally slowed.

But I had lost a tremendous amount of blood.

They decided I needed a blood transfusion.

Later, they found that not all of the tissue had passed. I would need a D&C the following day.

That night, my hospital room was full.

My family sat in chairs. Chris stayed close. People whispered, moved around, tried to be strong for me.

But I felt completely alone.

Alone in my body.

Alone in the loss.

Alone in the quiet space between what I hoped for and what was happening.

Grief settled in slowly, like a weight pressing on my chest. I couldn't breathe deeply. Everything inside me felt heavy and wrong.

The next day, before surgery, the doctors reminded me again: if I began bleeding uncontrollably, they would have to perform life-saving measures.

I closed my eyes.

"God, my life is Yours. My future is Yours. My womb is Yours."

The surgery went well. They were able to complete the procedure without a hysterectomy.

I was grateful. I truly was.

But gratitude and grief sat side by side inside me.

When I returned to my room, the emotions finally broke through. I cried for the baby I would never hold. For the future I had already imagined. For the hope that had felt so close.

Dr. O came up on his day off to check on me. He told me he and his wife had plans to see a play, but canceled to see me. That small act of care reminded me that even in loss, I was not unseen.

As the days passed, the weight did not lift. Before discharge, I needed one more blood transfusion. I waited for hours, exhausted and restless. When it finally came, it took hours more to complete.

Eventually, my levels stabilized.

I was discharged.

I went home.

And life kept moving forward, even though a part of me felt like it had stopped.

10

BRACE YOURSELF

***

Going home no longer pregnant left a silence I wasn't prepared for.

The house looked the same. The furniture hadn't moved. The air hadn't changed. But I had.

When I walked into my bathroom and saw the faint stain of blood still on the floor, my body reacted before my mind could form words. My chest tightened. My hands felt cold. I stood there longer than I meant to, staring at the place where everything had shifted.

It felt like my body remembered what my heart was still trying to process.

I felt empty. Not just physically, but spiritually. As if something sacred had passed through me and left a hollow space behind. The loss followed me from room to room, settling quietly in corners, waiting for me to acknowledge it.

On September 10, 2023, I was baptized at Chris's church.

Standing there in front of everyone, dressed in white, I felt exposed.

Not because of the people watching, but because I knew what I had just come through. I carried the memory of loss in my body. I carried the decision that had ended my pregnancy. I carried questions I had not yet learned how to answer.

When I stepped into the water, it was colder than I expected.

For a moment, I hesitated.

I wondered if God saw me the way I feared He did. I wondered if obedience still counted after everything that had happened. I wondered if I was clean.

Chris was smiling, his eyes steady and proud. His joy grounded me. I didn't fully understand what was happening in my spirit, but I knew something was shifting. I knew I didn't want to live the same way anymore.

When I went under the water, I closed my eyes.

For a brief second, everything was silent.

When I came back up, I didn't feel fireworks. I didn't feel instant peace. But I felt willing. And sometimes, willingness is where transformation begins.

After that, I spent a lot of time sitting alone with my thoughts. The house was quiet, and the quiet forced honesty out of me.

I realized I no longer wanted to stay in home care.

Truthfully, I had wanted to leave that job for a long time. But fear had kept me there. Fear of confrontation. Fear of financial instability. Fear of stepping into something unknown. I told myself I was staying for flexibility and money, but deep down, I knew I was also staying because it felt safer than starting over.

After the loss, something in me loosened.

When you walk through something that shakes your body and spirit, certain fears lose their grip.

I needed movement. I needed new air. I needed to feel like I was stepping toward something instead of standing still inside grief.

So, I applied for several jobs.

In October 2023, I interviewed for a leadership position. When they called me back for a second interview, I felt cautious hope. I didn't want to be disappointed. The next day, they offered me the job.

I remember sitting still after the phone call ended.

I didn't scream. I didn't jump. I just exhaled.

They told me it had come down to one other candidate and me. I didn't have the strongest résumé, they said, but I had something they couldn't train. Personality. Presence. Heart.

For the first time in a long time, I felt seen for something beyond survival.

I accepted with gratitude.

Putting in my thirty-day notice, however, exposed everything I had tolerated.

The stepfather tried to provoke me. His words were sharp, meant to draw a reaction. He questioned my character. He implied disloyalty. He wanted conflict.

But I didn't give it to him.

I listened. I asked him calmly if he was finished. And I completed my thirty days.

Obedience does not always look dramatic. Sometimes it looks like a restraint.

When I walked out on my last day, I didn't feel anger. I felt relief.

My mother later told me I should have left long before. She was probably right. But sometimes survival convinces us to endure what obedience would have told us to release sooner.

In November 2023, I began my new leadership role.

At first, I was excited. The environment felt kind. The pay was steady. It was something different. Something forward-moving.

Then one afternoon, during training and a staff meeting, my phone rang.

When I saw this department name on the screen, my stomach dropped.

It was connected to everything I thought I had already handled when I left. Everything I thought was finished.

I didn't answer.

Instead, I stepped outside and called someone I trusted who had faced something similar. As I explained what I saw, their voice began to tremble. They told me not to call the number back. They told me to get a lawyer immediately.

When someone else cries over your situation, you understand the gravity without explanation.

I contacted a lawyer that same day.

From that moment forward, my nervous system stayed on high alert. I checked my phone constantly. I replayed decisions in my head. I struggled to focus at work. I felt watched by something I couldn't see yet.

I wasn't just stressed.

I was bracing.

Around that same time, my hair began to fall out more noticeably.

The methotrexate, the low-dose chemotherapy used to end my pregnancy, was still working its way through my body. Hair loss was a side effect they had mentioned casually. It did not feel casual.

My hair had always been thick and full. It framed my face in a way that felt familiar. Watching it thin felt like losing another layer of myself.

Each time I brushed it, strands collected in the sink. In the shower. On my pillow.

It was a quiet grief layered on top of everything else.

In December 2023, I cut it to my shoulders.

It helped for a moment. It felt like action. But it did not stop the shedding.

Meanwhile, my new job grew heavier. Staffing shortages meant longer hours. If someone called off, I stayed. If coverage fell through, I adjusted. I was on call every day and every other weekend.

The role that once felt like an opportunity began to feel consuming.

And I was already tired.

So, I put in another thirty-day notice.

In January 2024, Chris and I went on vacation.

When I look back at the pictures now, I see something I didn't fully acknowledge then. My smile was present, but my eyes looked distant. I was trying. I was participating. But inside, I was carrying weight that the camera could not capture.

On January 31, 2024, I cut my hair again.

This time, completely short.

I sat in the chair and watched pieces of myself fall to the floor. I told myself it was practical.

That it was just hair, but it felt like surrender.

When I looked in the mirror afterward, I barely recognized myself.

I felt exposed. Vulnerable. Unhidden.

That evening, I went to Chris's house with my hood pulled up. My stomach tightened when he asked to see it.

Slowly, I pulled the hood down.

He looked at me for a moment and said, *"Oh my goodness, baby you look so beautiful."*

I felt something loosen in my chest.

Not because of vanity. Not because of appearance.

But because even stripped down physically, emotionally, and spiritually, I was still loved.

Through the loss. Through the uncertainty. Through the fear. Through the exhaustion.

He stayed.

And in a season where so much felt unstable, that steadiness mattered more than anything else.

11

MY NEW REALITY

***

When I went to church with Chris, I felt things deeply, sometimes in ways that made me uncomfortable. The preaching stirred something inside me that I did not yet have language for. It confronted areas of my heart I had managed to avoid for years. I was not used to a church that felt so intense, so reverent, so undeniably holy.

Instead of feeling soothed, I often felt exposed.

At first, I told myself that discomfort was growth. But over time, it became harder to sit through the services. I found myself bracing during sermons, anticipating conviction. I wasn't ready for that level of confrontation. Eventually, I stopped going.

One afternoon, feeling heavier than usual, I called my realtor, Kim, who had gradually become more than a business contact. She had become a friend. I told her everything. I spoke honestly about my confusion, my tension with Chris, the legal situation, and the fear that seemed to hum quietly in the background of my life.

She didn't interrupt. She prayed.

Her prayer was steady and sincere. It wasn't dramatic. It was grounding. I felt seen in a way that didn't feel condemning. Before we ended the call, she invited me to her husband's church. He was a pastor. I agreed to go.

And when I did, something shifted.

The atmosphere felt different. I wasn't overwhelmed. I wasn't bracing. I felt invited instead of confronted. For the first time, I wanted to learn on my own terms. I began reading the Bible privately, not because someone told me to, not to prove anything to Chris, but because I genuinely wanted understanding.

That decision marked the beginning of a faith that felt personal. It felt like mine.

But growth rarely happens without tension.

Leaving Chris's church created distance between us. He believed a couple should worship together. I understood that. But I also knew I needed space to grow without feeling pressured. The more I leaned into what I needed spiritually, the more unsettled our relationship became. Conversations felt strained. Small disagreements carried more weight than they should have.

Around that same time, my body began to change.

I gained weight, more than I ever had before—over thirty pounds. When I stepped on the scale and saw 166 pounds staring back at me, I barely recognized myself. My clothes fit differently. My energy felt different. I avoided mirrors some days.

Looking back, I know I was stress-eating. It was the only thing that felt immediate and comforting in a season where everything else felt uncertain. My relationship was fragile. My legal situation was looming. My future felt unstable.

Then my ears began to hurt.

The pain was subtle at first, then persistent. An audiologist confirmed hearing loss in both ears, more significant in my right. I sat there, trying to process the words. Hearing loss. At my age. It felt unfair. I remember thinking quietly, *why is all of this happening at once?*

Professionally, though, something good was unfolding.

I stepped into another leadership role and found that I loved it. I was trained as an instructor. I began teaching. I discovered confidence in communication and clarity in leadership. That job reminded me that I was capable, even when other areas of my life felt like they were unraveling.

But the legal situation never left my mind.

I stayed in constant communication with my lawyer. He explained the reality: restitution would be required. There would likely be something on my record. All because I had trusted someone without doing my own due diligence. I had believed what sounded legitimate. I had not asked enough questions.

I took responsibility.

Still, the consequences felt heavy. My career could be affected. My reputation could change. I began preparing for the worst. I saved aggressively. I minimized my expenses. I enrolled in real estate school as a backup plan. Completing the coursework felt like reclaiming a small measure of control.

In June 2024, Chris and I went on a cruise.

The ocean was beautiful. The air was warm. People around us laughed freely. I tried to enjoy it. I really did. But my court date was only weeks away. Even in the middle of open water, I felt confined by what was coming.

On July 17, 2024, I walked into a courtroom to hear my fate.

I cried on the drive there, but quietly. I was exhausted from crying. My lawyer did most of the talking. I listened as the judge explained the outcome.

When the words settled, I felt both relief and grief. Relief that it wasn't worse. Grief that my record would carry a mark I could not immediately erase.

Tears slid down my face in the courtroom anyway.

Before we left, my lawyer asked the judge if I could apply for expungement after a year. The judge agreed. I had never been in trouble before. That small mercy felt larger than it should have. It was a reminder that consequences can coexist with grace.

The following month, my daughter Mariah was turning sixteen. I had been saving to buy her first car. In the middle of rebuilding my own stability, I wanted to give her something solid.

I learned about car auctions and decided to try one. I bought a car for her, but I remembered she had always said she wanted a black one. So, I listed the car I purchased for sale on Facebook, planning to try again.

It sold almost immediately.

That surprised me.

More than that, it awakened something in me.

I went back to another auction. Then another. Every couple of weeks, I bought cars, cleaned them up, negotiated, and resold them. I studied the process. I learned what to look for. I learned what to avoid. I found satisfaction in the rhythm of it.

In a season where so much felt outside my control, this felt strategic. Disciplined. Intentional.

By then, I had left my job shortly after court. Selling cars became my only income. What began as a birthday plan for my daughter became a new source of provision.

When Mariah's birthday arrived, we celebrated with a hotel party and dinner the next day. I had Chris bring her car to the restaurant. When he arrived, we all walked outside together.

Her face lit up.

She was overwhelmed with joy. And watching her, I felt something shift inside me, too.

Even though Chris and I were still navigating tension, even though my life had changed in ways I had not planned, that moment felt pure.

It was proof that storms do not erase blessings.

Sometimes, they reveal new ways to build.

12

TRYING AGAIN

***

Life continued, even as I tried to understand what it was becoming.

I was no longer working as a nurse. That chapter of my life had closed quietly, without ceremony. Instead, I was flipping cars, managing what I could, stretching what I had, and asking God what else He wanted from me in this season. I needed movement. I needed something productive, something that made me feel like I was still building and not just surviving.

So, I made a decision. If I could not work the way I once had, I would use the time to finish what I started. I enrolled to complete my bachelor's degree in nursing.

School became my anchor. When everything else felt uncertain, assignments were clear. Deadlines were fixed. Grades were measurable. In the quiet hours of studying, I found structure again. I focused deeply. It gave me something solid to hold on to.

In December 2024, I finished my BSN.

It wasn't just a degree. It was proof that I could still move forward, even when parts of my life felt stalled.

During that time, Chris and I were still together, though fragile would have been the most honest word to describe us. We were trying—both of us. We made a decision to live holy. No drinking. No fornication. No cursing. We stripped away habits that had once been normal for us and replaced them with discipline.

It was not easy.

Obedience rarely is.

There were adjustments. There were moments of tension. There were quiet irritations that surfaced when comfort was removed. But we stayed committed because we believed it mattered. We believed God honored obedience.

Spiritually, though, we were still moving in different directions. I had been praying for God to send Chris to my church. He had been praying for God to send me back to his. Neither of us saw it as pride at the time. We thought we were standing firm in conviction.

But conviction without understanding can look a lot like stubbornness.

Eventually, something shifted in me. It did not happen dramatically. There was no lightning bolt moment. It was a quiet realization that I had been resisting something I did not fully understand.

During that time away from his church, I started reading my Bible differently. Slower. With questions instead of assumptions.

And I realized something humbling.

His pastor had never preached anything wrong.

This whole time, I had not been rejecting the truth. I had been rejecting what I did not yet understand. I had opinions without foundation. I had conviction without depth. I simply had not known the Word well enough to discern for myself.

I did not know what God required of us then.

But I know now.

So, I went back.

I returned to his church even though our relationship was still unsteady. I needed to follow truth wherever it led, not wherever I was most comfortable.

In January 2025, we broke up.

It was not explosive. It was exhausted. Two people standing at the edge of something fragile, realizing love alone was not enough to stabilize it.

I remember walking away that night feeling both strong and shattered. Strong because I knew I had done what I could. Shattered because losing him felt like losing my closest companion.

The breakup lasted two weeks.

But those two weeks felt like a century.

I talked to him every day. I saw him every day. Yet something had shifted. The label was gone. The security was gone.

I cried.

Not loud, dramatic crying. Quiet tears at night. Tears before logging into Zoom for church. Tears after praying, asking God why obedience sometimes felt so costly.

At the same time, I had just started school for my master's degree. My days were full of assignments and planning and future-building. My nights were heavy with emotion.

My life felt full and empty all at once.

During that same season, I decided to create a TikTok page. I was looking for a provision. Another stream of income. Another way to build something stable.

I prayed a simple prayer. *God, if this is in Your will, let it grow.*

For two weeks, nothing significant happened. I posted consistently. I learned. I adjusted. It felt like sowing seeds into quiet ground.

Then one day, I filmed a video of myself going to the auction.

And everything shifted.

The notifications started coming in faster than I could read them. Comments. Messages. Questions. Followers are increasing by the hour. I remember staring at my phone, almost in disbelief. I had asked God for provision. I had not expected it to arrive like this.

People wanted to know how the auction worked. How to bid. What mistakes to avoid. What to look for.

And I realized something.

I had knowledge that could help people.

So, I created an Auction Guide eBook. I poured everything I knew into it. The do's. The don'ts. The strategy. The mistakes I had learned from. I did not hold anything back.

And it did well. It still does.

What started as a quiet prayer for provision became a new stream of income and a new level of confidence.

It reminded me that God could bless the work of my hands, even in seasons when my heart felt bruised.

During those two weeks of separation, church was held on Zoom, so I did not see him. The following week, in-person service resumed.

I was nervous walking in. My heart was beating harder than I expected. I assumed he had moved on. I braced myself for distance.

But when I walked into the church, he was right there.

He walked straight toward me and wrapped me in a hug. There was no hesitation. He looked genuinely happy to see me, almost childlike in his relief. And I felt it too. Two weeks had felt like forever.

We talked. He told me he had made one of my favorite dishes, his macaroni and cheese, and asked if I wanted some.

Of course, I said yes.

I went over after church. We talked for hours. He told me how much he had missed me. How strange it felt not to talk to me. How bored he had been without me.

I told him the truth.

I had not been bored.

I had been crying.

That day, he told me he did not want to be without me ever again. He said he wanted to marry me.

I was happy. I loved him. I wanted that too.

The following Sunday, he took me to our Pastor and told him he wanted to marry me. Our Pastor paused. He knew we had just broken up. He asked, *"What changed?"*

Chris said that during the separation, he realized he did not want to live without me.

Our Pastor agreed to move forward but insisted on premarital counseling first.

Then he looked at me and said something that settled deeper than I let on in that moment.

"It's not you I'm worried about. It's him. He's too up and down."

I smiled politely. But inside, I felt the weight of that observation. It was not new information. It was confirmation of something I had quietly noticed but had not fully confronted. I tucked the words away, unsure whether they were caution or prophecy.

Valentine's Day came soon after. Chris bought me the most beautiful roses, with *I love you, Markiana* written across them. There was a card. Dinner reservations. Effort.

I felt happy. Relieved. Hopeful.

I started saving wedding hairstyles on my phone. I created a wedding song list in my notes. I allowed myself to imagine walking down an aisle. I let myself believe stability was finally within reach.

The following month was my graduation.

Standing there in my cap and gown, surrounded by my mom and her husband, Mariah, my brother Keith, Chris, and my grandpa, I felt something steady beneath me.

Pride. Gratitude. Grounding.

Even though my life was not fully settled, that moment reminded me of something important.

Forward is still forward, even when it is slow.

13

THE STORM CONTINUES...

***

March 2025 brought another blow.

Because of my record, the nursing board placed restrictions on my license for two years. It wasn't a suspension, but it felt like something worse, a visible mark. A reminder stamped across my professional identity. When I opened the notice and read the words, my stomach tightened. My hands went cold. I had already endured loss, legal consequences, career shifts, and financial uncertainty. I thought I had absorbed enough impact.

But the storm wasn't finished.

It felt like every month arrived carrying its own test, as if I barely had time to steady myself before the next wave hit.

I cried that night. Not loud, dramatic tears, just quiet ones that slid down my face while I sat on the edge of my bed. I asked God questions I didn't say out loud during the day.

"Why does it keep stacking?"

"How much more refining do I need?"

And yet, even through the confusion, I kept praying. I kept thanking Him. Not because I felt strong, but because gratitude was the only discipline I could control. When everything else felt unstable, worship felt like something solid.

There was one song that carried me during that season, *Turning Around for Me* by VaShawn Mitchell. I played it over and over. Every time it came on, I cried. Not because I believed everything was turning around yet, but because I was trying to. I was trying to anchor my heart to hope before I could see evidence of it.

Somewhere in that season, I noticed something subtle but significant. The music I listened to changed completely. R&B faded out. Gospel filled the silence. The lyrics became lifelines. When people didn't know what to say to me, the music did. It held me together in ways conversations couldn't.

Then April came.

Mariah and I had a disagreement that grew faster and heavier than I expected. She told me I had been mean to her. That I was taking what I was going through out on her.

Her words caught me off guard. My first instinct was to defend myself. I told her I was carrying a lot. I told her she needed to listen when I asked her to do something. I told her how exhausting it was to repeat myself every day.

But even as I spoke, I could hear the tension in my own voice. I was tired. Not just physically. Soul tired. And maybe she had been absorbing more of that than I realized.

Later that afternoon, she came home from school. Her eyes were red before she even said anything. We tried talking again. This time, there were more tears than words.

"I'm going to live with my dad for a while," she said.

I didn't take her seriously. She had never lived with him. They didn't talk often. I assumed it was emotion speaking.

I was wrong.

About an hour later, I heard her bedroom door open. I looked up from the couch and saw her coming down the stairs with large bags in her hands. The sound of the wheels bumping against each step echoed through the house. She wasn't crying now. She looked determined.

Something inside me wanted to stop her. To say, *"Wait. Let's fix this."* But another part of me refused to beg.

I had spent so much of my life trying to hold everything together. In that moment, I didn't have the strength to hold her, either.

So, I stayed composed. My voice was steady when I told her to call me when she got there. I let her leave with dignity.

But when the door closed behind her, the silence hit me like a wave.

I collapsed onto the couch and sobbed. Not the quiet tears from before. These were loud. Unfiltered. The kind that leaves your chest aching.

I called her dad because I hadn't even spoken to him about this decision. He said it was fine for her to come. During that call, I learned something that cut even deeper. Mariah had told him and his sister everything I had been going through.

That was my personal business. I had asked her not to share it.

I felt exposed. Betrayed. Not just as a mother, but as a woman who had trusted her child with adult pain.

She stayed with her dad for about three weeks. Three weeks that felt endless.

Since I was nineteen, it had always been the two of us. Every decision. Every milestone. Every storm. We faced them side by side. Her absence changed the atmosphere of the house.

It was too quiet. No music from her room. No random conversations in the kitchen. No movement.

I didn't just miss her presence. I missed the version of myself that existed in proximity to her. Being her mother had structured my days, my purpose, my identity. Without her there, I felt unanchored.

During that time, I was with Chris almost every day. And almost every day, I cried. I tried not to. I didn't want to seem fragile. But the tears came anyway. He did his best to comfort me, to remind me that things would settle. But nothing quieted the ache. I felt like I had failed her somehow. Like I had let the storm seep into my parenting.

Eventually, she came home.

We sat down and talked not to defend, but to understand. It wasn't perfect. There were pauses. There were guarded moments. But it was a start. Healing didn't happen overnight, but effort did. And effort mattered.

Then May came.

It was Chris's birthday month, but somewhere along the way, something between us had shifted. Again.

He had stood beside me through loss, legal stress, and financial strain. He had helped me when I needed it most. But I could sense a quiet distance forming. It wasn't loud. It wasn't confrontational. It was subtle, like someone slowly loosening their grip.

I think the uncertainty of my future began to scare him. Not everyone knows how to love someone in transition. Not everyone can sit in instability without needing guarantees.

I remember one conversation clearly. I told him to have faith. I told him God would work everything out for me and for us. He agreed. At least verbally. But his eyes didn't match his words.

For his birthday, I took him out to dinner. I tried to make it special. But something felt different. He was present physically, but emotionally somewhere else.

On May 18, 2025, we were lying in bed talking about the fact that we had been celibate for eight months. Eight months of discipline. Eight months of trying to honor God. Eight months of choosing obedience over impulse.

I brought up marriage.

He paused.

It wasn't dramatic. He didn't argue. He didn't dismiss the idea. But his face shifted just slightly. Hesitation. Uncertainty. A flicker of doubt.

And immediately, my pastor's words echoed in my mind.

"It's not you I'm worried about. It's him because he's too up and down."

That sentence returned like a warning I had filed away but never fully processed.

In that moment, something inside me didn't break in anger; it clarified.

I realized I was tired of bracing myself. Tired of emotional instability. Tired of hoping someone would rise to consistency.

So, I said it plainly. If you're unsure, maybe we should end it now.

He agreed.

The finality of that agreement stunned me. I left his house feeling hollow. Hours later, I saw him at church. I didn't speak. I sat there wrestling with disbelief. Part of me still thought we would circle back. That love would override hesitation. Those eight months of discipline meant something permanent.

But sometimes storms don't just test what you have.

They reveal what was never built to withstand the pressure.

14

THE BREAKUP

***

At first, the breakup felt like anger.

When I saw him at church, I didn't speak. If he spoke to me, I responded politely, but without warmth. I kept my distance and told myself I was protecting my peace. I convinced myself that silence was strength.

But as the weeks passed, the anger softened and the ache settled in.

At night, when the house grew quiet and there was nothing to distract me, the grief would rise. I would lie in bed staring at the ceiling, replaying conversations in my mind. The way he used to pray with me. The way we laughed over small things. I believed, without question, that he was my husband.

I truly believed that.

He had been my best friend. We did everything together. Every routine carried his memory. Every Sunday felt incomplete. And the more time passed, the harder it became to pretend I was unaffected.

I prayed about it often. I asked God to take the ache away if it was not His will. Some nights, I asked for restoration. Other nights, I asked for clarity. What I did not realize at the time was that I was still holding onto hope while asking God for peace. And you cannot fully receive one while gripping the other.

By July, my mom could see it written all over me.

She told me she wanted to take me to Las Vegas to visit family, just to get me out of the house and into a different environment. At first, I told her I didn't want to go. I didn't have the emotional energy to be "on." But she insisted, and eventually I agreed.

While I was there, I tried my best to show up. I smiled. I got dressed. I sat at dinner tables and listened to conversations. But there was a heaviness I couldn't shake. My mom grew a little frustrated at first because she felt like I wasn't fully enjoying myself. I had to explain that I was doing the best I could. I was carrying more than she could see. I was still grieving and still processing and still untangling hope from reality.

Once she understood that, she softened.

One night in Vegas, I stayed up talking with my twin cousin, Jessica. The house was quiet, and the conversation stretched into the early hours of the morning.

I shared everything that had happened over the last two years, the prayers, the waiting, the disappointment, the discipline, the obedience.

As I talked, her eyes filled with tears.

She couldn't believe how much I had endured silently. She told me, strongly, that I needed to write a book. She said my story wasn't just a relationship story; it was about faith under pressure.

That conversation planted something in me.

For the first time, I considered that maybe the storm had a purpose.

While in Vegas, it felt good to get dressed up again. Back home, I wasn't going anywhere except church and the grocery store. Being out with family gave me a reason to put on nice clothes, to do my hair, to feel like myself again.

But even that had changed.

I no longer wore crop tops or short outfits. I had given away much of that clothing and replaced it with modest pieces. The shift hadn't been forced. No one pressured me. It happened quietly, naturally, as my relationship with God deepened. My outside began to reflect what was happening internally.

When I looked in the mirror, I didn't just see a woman recovering from heartbreak. I saw a woman refining herself—a woman choosing alignment over attention. A woman walking differently.

I felt like a holy woman of God.

When I returned home, something shifted again.

At the beginning of August 2025, Chris started being friendlier toward me at church. He initiated a conversation. He hugged me. He told me he loved me and kissed me on the cheek.

I didn't show it outwardly, but inside, hope flared.

I wondered quietly if this was restoration. I wondered if maybe God had been working on both of us separately. I didn't say it aloud, but in my heart I thought, *maybe this is how it comes back.*

We began talking more outside of church. Eventually, he invited me over. The first time I went back to his house, he asked me how it felt to be reconnected.

"It feels great," I told him honestly.

When I asked how he felt, he said it felt good and then added, almost casually, that if we got back together, cool… and if we didn't, cool.

That sentence lingered.

It sounded light. Detached. Optional.

I told him I felt the same way, but the truth was, I thought I did. I wanted to believe I could be that casual. That uninvested. That's free.

But my heart was not casual.

We went on a date. I was nervous, but we had a good time. For a moment, it felt like we were finding our rhythm again. I allowed myself to relax. I allowed myself to imagine.

Then, toward the end of August, something small exposed something bigger.

After church one Sunday, we were on the phone. I mentioned how I used to swim a certain way when I was younger. He insisted it was impossible. I laughed at first, thinking he was joking. But he grew irritated, firm in correcting me about my own memory.

"It doesn't work like that," he said.

I explained again. He dismissed it.

What began as a minor difference turned into tension. His tone shifted. Sharp. Final. And suddenly, the call ended.

It was small.

But it wasn't.

It wasn't about swimming.

It was about being heard.

It was about how quickly something light could become heavy, about how disagreement turned into irritation instead of understanding.

That same day, we celebrated Mariah's birthday. Even after the earlier disagreement, he came over to celebrate. We sang. We cut the cake. We smiled for pictures.

But something felt different.

The warmth had thinned.

After he went home, the calls became less frequent. The tone softened into distance. The effort changed not dramatically, but noticeably.

And this time, I didn't chase clarity.

My master's graduation was on September 6, 2025. Instead of doing something big, I chose a simple brunch with my mom, Mariah, Chris, and his child.

We ate. We talked. We smiled.

But inside, I was watching.

Watching the gaps in conversation.

Watching the emotional distance.

Watching myself detach.

That was the last day we spent time together.

There wasn't a dramatic ending. No explosion. No final speech.

Just distance.

And this time, I felt it clearly.

Not just the loss, but the lesson.

Peace does not return to what once disturbed it.

And obedience sometimes means letting go twice.

15

REALITY SET IN

***

About two weeks after my graduation, reality met me head-on.

I was at church when I saw Chris standing a few rows ahead of me, showing something on his phone to a couple of people. I wasn't trying to listen, but his voice carried just enough for me to hear him say he was going to have a visitor coming.

A visitor.

My stomach dropped.

The room felt smaller. Louder. Heavier. The worship music kept playing, people kept smiling, but everything inside me went still.

How could you move on so quickly?

How could you announce it so openly while I was standing in the same room?

How could you say you loved me... and look so unaffected?

I tried to keep my face neutral. I lifted my hands during worship as I had done so many times before.

But my chest felt tight, like something was pressing against it from the inside. My palms were cold. My thoughts were racing, but my body felt frozen.

By the time service ended, I walked out as calmly as I could. The second my car door shut, I broke.

That kind of hurt feels physical. It sits in your chest. It steals your breath. I gripped the steering wheel and sobbed, not the quiet tears you wipe away quickly, but the kind that shake your whole body. The finality of it hit me all at once.

It was over.

Not complicated. Not delayed. Not "maybe someday."

Over.

There would be no circling back. No, "we just need time." No quiet reconciliation months later, when emotions cooled, he was moving forward publicly.

And I had to accept that.

Acceptance didn't feel strong. It felt like surrendering something I had prayed over, hoped for, imagined differently. It felt like letting go of a future I had already started building in my mind.

I didn't want to let it go.

But obedience sometimes means releasing what you love, even when you don't understand why.

The days that followed were heavy. I went through the motions, church, and conversations, but everything felt muted. I prayed, but some prayers were just silence. I didn't ask God to fix it anymore. I asked Him to steady me.

And then, just as one door closed loudly in my heart, another opened quietly in my life.

On September 23, 2025, I was driving to a friend's daughter's birthday party when I randomly thought about my lawyer. July 17, 2025, marked one full year since my record. He had told me to reach back out at the end of July, and I did. He filed my expungement application on August 2, 2025.

He said it would likely take about a month to hear something, then another month to go to court. We were probably looking at October.

September had come and gone quietly. I hadn't heard anything about a court date.

While driving to the party, I felt a nudge to text him.

Nothing dramatic. Just a thought that wouldn't leave.

So, I sent the message.

I tried to be present at the party. I smiled. I made small talk. I watched children run around laughing, full of lightness I didn't quite feel. After about thirty minutes, my phone rang.

It was him.

My heart started racing immediately. Not excitement, anxiety. I stepped outside, where it was quieter, and answered.

"I wanted to call you personally and tell you this," he said.

I braced myself.

He told me he had checked his email and that the judge had approved my expungement.

I paused, trying to process what he just said.

"Okay... so when is the court date?"

He hesitated. *"There is no court date. Let me read it to you."*

He read the official language. My expungement had been approved. There were no criminal proceedings against me.

No court appearance. No waiting. No additional process.

Just approved.

For a second, I couldn't speak. It felt unreal, like my mind was trying to catch up to what my ears had just heard.

And then I broke down.

But this time, the tears weren't from loss.

They were from release.

My shoulders dropped. My breathing changed. It felt like something invisible had finally lifted off me. The weight I had carried quietly, the shame, the limitation, the reminder of a mistake, was gone.

Even my lawyer sounded surprised. He explained that normally, you apply, receive a court date, appear before the judge, and then wait for approval. He had never experienced a case that bypassed the court altogether.

I listened to him explain the process, but inside, something else was happening.

I replayed the nights I had cried—the mornings I chose discipline. The moments I had wanted to give up, but didn't. The prayers I prayed when no one was watching. The times I asked God to help me live right, not just look right.

And in that quiet space, I knew.

This wasn't coincidence.

This wasn't luck.

This wasn't favored by people.

This was God.

Not because everything had suddenly become perfect. Not because the heartbreak disappeared. But because in the middle of loss, He was still moving.

After everything, the loss, the license restrictions, the breakup, the weight gain, the sleepless nights, the uncertainty, God was reminding me that He had not forgotten me.

He was not silent.

He was not distant.

He was not done.

The heartbreak didn't disappear overnight. I still had moments of sadness. Still had questions. Still had to choose obedience daily.

But for the first time in a long time, I felt something stronger than fear.

I felt covered.

Not by circumstances.

Not by relationships.

Not by outcomes.

By grace.

And grace felt like peace settling where panic used to live.

16

PAIN, PURPOSE, STRENGTH

***

Even after my expungement was approved, it didn't feel real.

On paper, I was cleared. Officially free. The weight that had followed me for a year was legally lifted.

But internally, I was still carrying so much.

I was relieved. Grateful. Lighter in one area of my life. For the first time in a long time, I could see a small light at the end of the tunnel.

But healing is rarely linear.

Every time I thought about Chris being with someone else, my stomach would tighten so suddenly it felt like I had missed a step in the dark. My anxiety wasn't occasional. It was constant. It sat in my chest like pressure. I would cry without warning. Driving. Sitting in my room. Folding clothes that still held memories.

And every Sunday, as I prepared for church, my chest would tighten before I even left the house.

I would sit in my car in the parking lot for a few extra minutes, gripping the steering wheel.

Is this the day I see him with someone else?

The anticipation was sometimes worse than the reality. My mind would race ahead of me, creating scenes before they even happened. I cried out to God constantly. I fasted. I journaled pages filled with questions. I prayed until I had no more words left, and then I prayed again, even when it felt like heaven was quiet.

People outside the church told me to leave.

"Why would you keep putting yourself through that?" they asked.

And for a moment, that sounded like relief.

But I couldn't leave.

Even though he brought me there, it was no longer just his church. It had become mine. I believed God led me there. And I refused to let heartbreak uproot what God planted in my life.

So, I stayed.

With tears in my eyes.

With pain in my chest.

With a heart that felt bruised but still beating.

During that season, I lost so much weight I barely recognized myself. I dropped down to 127 pounds. My clothes hung differently. My face looked sharper in the mirror. I barely had an appetite. Grief will do that. Anxiety will do that.

But I kept going.

I am forever grateful for my pastor and the few people who quietly encouraged me to push through. They didn't demand explanations. They didn't tell me to "get over it." They simply reminded me to keep standing.

After my record was expunged, I began applying for nursing jobs again. Each application felt like reclaiming a piece of myself. When I landed an interview for a school nurse position, hope stirred in me for the first time in months.

During the interview, the recruiter asked if I had any restrictions on my license.

I told her yes.

She asked what they were. I explained. She looked them up herself and told me the restrictions would not affect this particular role.

She wanted to hire me.

I walked out of that building feeling seen. Capable. Useful again.

She told me she would inform upper management about my restrictions and that once my background check cleared, we would move forward. I completed my background check that same day.

The following week, I received my official offer letter.

I started working, and I loved it.

I loved being around the children. I loved the routine. I loved hearing little footsteps in the hallway and being the calm place they ran to when they didn't feel well. I loved feeling useful again. Purposeful.

For a moment, it felt like restoration.

But once I got comfortable, I followed up with the recruiter and asked if she had spoken with management about my restrictions.

She hadn't.

My stomach dropped in a way that felt familiar. That sinking feeling of something good slipping away.

That conversation was supposed to happen before I even started.

She said she would speak with them immediately. Later, she called and asked me to send over my restriction paperwork because the manager wanted to review it.

Her voice sounded uneasy.

By the end of my shift, the Human Resources manager called me and told me not to report back to work until they completed their review.

I remember staring at my phone after the call ended. Sitting in silence and trying to prepare myself for what I already felt coming.

The next day, they called again.

They decided not to keep me. They didn't want to do the additional work to ensure compliance.

My heart cracked, but not the way it once would have.

The old me might have spiraled and questioned my worth and questioned God.

This time, I exhaled.

It hurt. Deeply. But I also knew something was shifting inside of me. Disappointment no longer destroyed me. It refined me.

Meanwhile, my TikTok eBook was still selling. I had added one-on-one auction mentorship sessions for people who wanted to learn directly from me. That income continued to sustain me.

God was still providing.

And that experience reminded me of something important: nursing is my calling.

After the restrictions were placed on my license, I had almost walked away from nursing altogether. I even changed my master's program from nursing to business, trying to protect myself from more rejection.

But working as a school nurse, even briefly, reminded me how much I love caring for others. It wasn't just a job. It was part of who I am.

December 2025 arrived, the holidays, and my birthday.

The breakup pain was still there, but something inside me was steadier. Not healed yet. But steadier. I was waking up every day thankful, even in the storm. My relationship with God was growing deeper in ways I couldn't fully explain.

Our church was preparing for a Christmas event, and the day before the service, my pastor called and asked if I would do the scripture reading.

I was ecstatic.

I had been praying for God to help me step out of my shyness, to allow me to testify and sing without the butterflies, to be used in the church despite everything I was carrying.

And here was the opportunity.

That Sunday, my hands trembled slightly as I walked to the front. But my voice did not.

When the pastor called me up, I read the scripture confidently. Not because I wasn't nervous, but because God had been strengthening me quietly all along.

My church family was proud. My pastor was proud.

And for the first time in a long time, I was proud of myself.

After service, we had a small Christmas gathering. The women served food to visitors first, then to members.

Toward the end of serving, I saw Chris step outside.

My heart immediately began pounding.

I knew the moment I had been dreading was here.

When he came back in, he wasn't alone.

For a split second, my vision blurred. I thought I might vomit.

But I held it together.

When he came through the line to get food, I placed his chicken on his plate a little harder than necessary.

That was the extent of my reaction.

And I was proud of that.

Because what I wanted to do was far worse than what my flesh wanted.

All I could think about was how in August we were reconnecting, and by October, he was in something else entirely.

That realization sliced through me in a way I can't fully describe.

I stayed composed inside the building and smiled when necessary— kept serving.

But once I got to my car, I broke down.

The parking lot lights glowed through my tears. My breathing became shallow. My heart felt like it was collapsing inward.

I cried in a way that had no sound at first, just shaking.

"I don't want him back," I whispered. *"I just want peace."*

Christmas arrived.

I host Christmas at my home. For the last two years, he had helped me.

This year, I did it alone.

I cooked. I smiled. I served my family.

Outwardly, I was composed.

But inwardly, I was carrying grief like a quiet companion.

After everyone left, my mom texted me. She told me it hurt her to see me sad. Even though I wasn't crying in front of them, they could see the pain in my eyes.

She told me she was going to pray for me that God would help me get over this situation.

I thanked her.

Then I cried out to God again.

Not asking for him back.

Not asking for explanations.

Just asking for peace. For a healed heart. For the strength to let go without becoming bitter.

And that prayer didn't change my circumstances.

It changed me.

17

COMMIT THY WAY

***

"Commit thy way unto the Lord; trust in Him; and He shall bring it to pass.

And He shall bring forth thy righteousness as the light, and thy judgment as the noonday."— Psalm 37:5–6

December 26, the day after Christmas, was my birthday dinner.

I had my makeup professionally done. I ordered a beautiful, blue sequin-colored dress that felt soft against my skin. I even booked a photographer to take pictures of my two close friends and me before dinner. When I stepped in front of the camera, I didn't feel like I was trying to prove anything. I just felt present.

When I looked in the mirror, I felt good.

Not just physically, but internally. There was no heaviness behind my eyes. No silent ache sitting in my chest. Just calm.

Dinner was peaceful. We laughed, the kind of laughter that makes your stomach tighten and your mascara threaten to run.

At one point, one of my friends reached across the table, squeezed my hand, and said, *"Look at you. You made it."* And I realized I had.

We reflected. We talked about growth, about how much had changed in such a short amount of time. There were tears, but they weren't heavy tears. They were grateful ones. The kind that fall when you know you survived something that once felt like it would take you out.

For the first time in a long time, I felt light.

The next day, on my actual birthday, I hosted a small gathering at my house. We all wore matching pajamas. My daughter laughed as we tried to take group pictures, everyone talking at once, adjusting sleeves, fixing hair. We played games, ate food and cake, and sang happy birthday.

I laughed the entire day.

When I look back at the pictures, I see joy. Real joy. Not forced. Not pretending. Not me trying to convince myself I was okay.

I was okay.

That was God.

Because months before, I could barely breathe from heartbreak. I remember nights when the silence felt suffocating.

When my prayers sounded more like sobs than sentences. And now, here I was, smiling without effort.

That wasn't coincidence. That was healing.

I brought in the New Year 2026 at home on Zoom with my church, just like I had the past few years. But this time felt different. I wasn't praying for survival. I wasn't asking God to fix something. I wasn't bargaining.

I was simply thankful.

In past years, my faith had been reactive. I would run to God when something hurt. I would fast when something broke. I would pray intensely when I was afraid of losing something.

But this time, I wasn't in crisis.

I was consistent.

I was praying because I loved Him. Reading because I wanted to hear Him. Fasting because I desired discipline. My relationship with God was no longer built on emergency; it was built on intimacy.

I was excited for the New Year.

I didn't know what was coming, but I trusted that whatever it was, it would be intentional.

I was working on my book and feeling stronger mentally and emotionally. I continued praying, reading my Bible, journaling, fasting, attending church, Bible study, and working out. Not because I was trying to escape pain, but because I was building a lifestyle.

And in the stillness, I began to hear Him more clearly.

God told me to be still.

Not because nothing was happening.

But because everything was aligning.

So that's what I've been doing.

Being still.

Pouring into myself.

Loving myself.

Loving my daughter.

This is her senior year. We're preparing for prom, senior pictures, and graduation, and it still hasn't fully hit me. She's going to college. She'll live on campus. I'll be an empty nester.

Since I was nineteen, it has always been us.

Every decision.

Every struggle.

Every celebration.

Every storm.

Now, soon, it will just be me and Autumn, my one-year-old dog, in the house.

Sometimes I walk past her bedroom and pause. I imagine the quiet. I imagine the stillness of a house that once echoed with her laughter. It feels bittersweet. I'm proud of the woman she's becoming. But I am also learning who I am outside of being needed every day.

My baby has grown up.

And in many ways, so have I.

I am still navigating life, still learning, and still growing.

But I see things much clearer now.

Storms don't just destroy.

Sometimes they reveal what was unstable.

Sometimes they strip away what was never meant to stay.

And sometimes, they uncover strength you didn't know you possessed.

The storm didn't break me.

It built discipline.

It built boundaries.

It built discernment.

It built a deeper obedience.

It built a quieter, steadier faith.

It positioned me exactly where I was meant to stand all along.

And now, when the winds rise again, because they always do, I know I will not be moved the same way.

Because I am no longer trying to survive the storm.

I am standing in who I became because of it.

18

WHAT THE STORM REVEALED

***

What I realized through this storm is that nothing I endured was wasted.

Not the humiliation. Not the anxiety. Not the silence. Not the nights I cried myself to sleep, wondering how everything unraveled so quickly.

There was purpose in all of it.

Before everything fell apart, I was a good person by most standards. I loved hard. I worked hard. I provided. I achieved. From the outside, my life looked full.

But I was still worldly.

I idolized money. I cared deeply about image. I equated success with security. I prayed, but I was not surrendered. I believed in God, but I had not truly submitted to Him.

I did not know His Word the way I thought I did. I did not understand obedience beyond convenience.

I was partying. Fornicating. Living in ways that felt normal at the time. Justified. Accepted and applauded, even.

But God had a calling on my life.

And sometimes when God calls you higher, the ground beneath you begins to shift. What feels stable starts to crack. What feels secure begins to loosen.

He prunes.

He strips.

He removes what cannot go where He is taking you.

If I am honest, I would not be the woman I am today without the loss. Without the heartbreak. Without the legal trouble. Without the embarrassment that forced me to sit still. Without the loneliness that confronted me with myself.

Those things disciplined me.

They humbled me.

They brought me to my knees.

And in that position, I finally learned how to stay there willingly.

I remember one night after everything ended with my relationship. The house was quiet. Too quiet. I had already explained to friends why I needed to walk away. I had already convinced myself it was the right decision.

But obedience does not always feel victorious in the moment.

It felt like grief.

I sat on the edge of my bed and whispered, *"God, if this is You, give me the strength to let it go."*

There was no audible voice. No dramatic sign. Just a steady peace that did not argue back. A calm that settled deeper than emotion.

And I knew.

Even though we had stopped fornicating, I was still trying to be a wife to a man who was not my husband. I was emotionally submitting without a covenant and giving what belonged under covering.

God corrected me gently, but firmly.

Submit fully to Me first.

Submission belongs to God and to a husband. I had love, but I did not have alignment. I did not have a covenant. And love without alignment will eventually wound you.

Letting go hurt.

But holding on would have cost me more.

As I write this, I have been celibate for eighteen months. I have not had a drink of alcohol in twenty months. There were moments early on when temptation whispered. When loneliness tried to convince me that compromise would be easier.

But something inside me had shifted.

My desires changed.

My language changed.

My pace changed.

I do not move the way I used to. I no longer rush ahead trying to control outcomes. I seek God first. I wait longer. I listen more closely.

I hear Him now, not audibly, but through conviction. Through restraint. Through unexpected peace, when I choose obedience.

During this journey, I learned patience. I learned contentment. I learned how to call on the Lord daily, not just when everything collapses.

There were seasons when I kept yearning for more. A bigger house. More money. More visible success. I thought achievement would quiet the restlessness inside me.

It never did.

Because the void I was trying to fill was spiritual, not material.

That void was God.

Now, even though I do not have as much materially as I once did, I feel more complete than I ever have. Not because my circumstances are perfect, but because my foundation is different.

God truly supplies every need, according to His will.

Even my pregnancy, the most traumatic experience of my life, was not random.

I had prayed for another child. I wanted one. I believed I was ready. But God saw what I could not see. He saw the legal battles ahead. The instability. The emotional toll I would carry.

Deep down, I had always said that if I had another child, I wanted it to be within covenant, within covering.

What felt like loss was protection.

What felt like heartbreak was mercy.

Some things feel like loss, but are actually divine interruption.

If I could leave you with anything, it would be this:

God sometimes separates before He elevates.

Pain can move you closer to purpose than comfort ever could.

Restoration often begins quietly, long before anyone else sees it.

And peace usually waits on obedience.

"We make our plans, but the Lord determines our steps." (Proverbs 16:9)

Today, my mornings look different. I wake up without striving. I open my Bible before I open my phone. I sit in silence without fear of what silence might reveal.

There is no chaos in my spirit anymore.

The storm did not destroy me.

It revealed me.

It revealed what I had built on sand.

It revealed who I was when everything external was stripped away.

And though I would never ask to relive that pain, I would not trade the woman it shaped me into.

I lost things.

I lost people.

I lost illusions.

But I gained obedience.

I gained discipline.

I gained peace.

And most of all, I gained intimacy with God.

The storm did not end my story.

It redirected it.

And for that, I am grateful.

About The Author

***

Markiana Cornist is a woman whose life has been transformed through faith, perseverance, and obedience to God. Her journey has been marked by seasons of joy, unexpected trials, heartbreak, restoration, and spiritual growth. Through it all, she has learned that storms are not meant to destroy us; they are meant to shape us.

As a nurse, entrepreneur, mother, and woman of faith, she has experienced firsthand what it means to be stretched beyond her comfort zone and still choose trust. Her story is not one of perfection, but of surrender: learning to release control, lean on God's promises, and move forward even when the path is unclear.

She is deeply passionate about encouraging women to trust God in every season, remain disciplined in their faith, and understand that even painful chapters can lead to purpose. Her prayer is that her testimony reminds others that healing is possible, peace is attainable, and God's plans are always greater than our own.

The Perfect Storm is her first book and a reflection of the strength that can be found when faith becomes the foundation of one's life.